First Facts®

CURIOUS SCIENTISTS

T0044856

EXCITING ENGINEERING ACTIVITIES

by Angie Smibert

CAPSTONE PRESS
a capstone imprint

First Facts are published by Capstone Press,
1710 Roe Crest Drive, North Mankato, Minnesota 56003
www.mycapstone.com

Library of Congress Cataloging-in-Publication Data
Cataloging-in-Publication data is available on the Library of Congress website.
ISBN 978-1-5157-6884-5 (library binding)
ISBN 978-1-5157-6890-6 (paperback)
ISBN 978-1-5157-6902-6 (eBook PDF)

Editorial Credits
Anna Butzer, editor; Heidi Thompson, designer; Kelly Garvin, media researcher; Laura
Manthe, production specialist

Photo Credits
All photos are shot by the Capstone Studio, Karon Dubke

Artistic Elements
Shutterstock: amgun, (gears) design element throughout

TABLE OF CONTENTS

THINKING BIG

Do you often wonder how the objects around you work? When you're stuck in traffic on a bridge, do you wonder how the bridge is holding all those cars? When the traffic light ahead changes, do you wonder how it works?

An engineer is behind all of these amazing inventions. They design, build, and test products and structures we use every day. Some engineers design and build machines and robots. Others design buildings or work with electricity. Sound amazing? You can be an engineer too! With this book, you'll get to build bridges and buildings, make circuits, and even create a water filter. And the results will be awesome!

Safe Science

Read through each activity before starting. Collect all of the materials that you will need. You may need an adult to help you find or buy some materials. Experiments can be tricky. Be sure to ask an adult for help if you need it.

DOME EGG-SPERIMENT

Eggs just might be nature's most perfect package. A chick can easily crack the shell with its tiny beak. Its shape can support the weight of the hen — plus a lot more! Let's see how much pressure eggs can take before cracking!

Materials:

- 2 eggs (raw)
- container (for yolks and whites)
- paper towel
- several hardcover books

Steps:

1. Carefully crack each egg in half around the middle. Set aside the pointy-shaped halves. Put the yolks and whites in a container and refrigerate them. You won't need these for the experiment, but you can save them for breakfast or bake with them.
2. Rinse and dry the remaining egg halves. You should have four, **dome**-shaped halves left.
3. With the dome side up, place the eggshells on a flat surface. They should be in a square and evenly spaced.
4. Lay a book on top of the eggs. How much weight do you think the eggshells can hold?
5. Keep adding books until the egg shells crack!

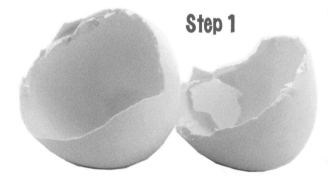

Step 1

How it Works:

You were probably surprised by how many books the egg shells were able to support. It's all in the egg's shape: the dome. You've probably seen it used in buildings, such as the United States Capitol. Many sports stadiums have domes too. A dome can hold up a heavy load. Its shape evenly divides weight.

dome—a structure shaped like half of a ball

PAPER AND PENCIL CIRCUIT

In a flashlight **electricity** travels from a power source to a light bulb through copper wires. The path the electricity follows is called a circuit. But you don't need wires to make a circuit. You can actually draw one on paper!

Materials:

- graphite pencil, 2B or higher
  (You can find these at an art supply store.)
- paper
- ruler
- LED light (5mm)
- 9-volt battery
- clear tape

Steps:

1. Use your pencil to draw a simple design on a piece of paper. Draw a circle, square, or a zig-zag line as shown. This will be the path of your circuit. Make the lines thick for the best results.
2. Leave a small gap, about 1 centimeter, in the line on both the right and left sides of the drawing. (You can erase the line.) The battery and light will go in these gaps.

Step 2

3. Take the ends of the LED light and separate them a bit. Tape the ends of the LED to the lines on the right side of the page. The light bulb should be in the gap.

4. Place the 9-volt battery upside down in the gap on the left side of the drawing. The battery's positive and negative terminal should each touch one of the lines. You may need to move the battery around to get the terminals to line up. The LED should light up.

5. Play around with different circuit designs. Does the length or width of the line make a difference in how brightly the light shines? Can you add more LEDs?

How it Works:

Graphite is an electrical **conductor**. A conductor is a material that electricity can travel through. Not all conductors are alike. Copper is a better conductor than graphite. That's why electrical wires are often made out of copper.

electricity—flow or stream of charged particles, such as electrons

conductor—a material or object that allows electricity or heat to move through it

TRUSS BRIDGE

Bridges carry tons of weight every day. One of the oldest designs is called a **truss** bridge. A truss uses triangles to make the structure strong. How strong is a truss bridge? You're about to find out!

Materials:

- craft sticks (30-50)
- glue
- zip ties (10-20)
- rope (1-2 feet)
- 2 chairs (or other level surfaces)
- weights

Steps:

A truss bridge has three parts: two sides and a bottom. Each side is a series of overlapping triangles.

1. Glue three craft sticks together to form a triangle.
2. Glue two more sticks on the right side to form an upside down triangle.

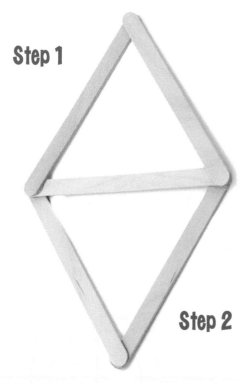

Step 1

Step 2

truss—a structure made up of connecting triangles

3. Glue two more sticks to form a right-side up triangle. Repeat steps 2 and 3 until you have three triangles across the bottom and two across the top. This is one side.

4. Repeat the above steps to make the other side of the truss. Make sure all the sticks along the bottom are straight.

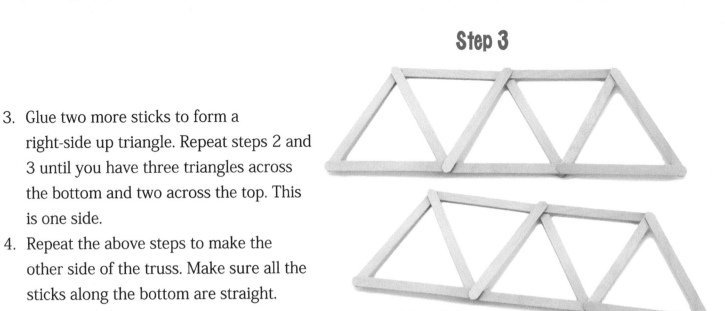

Step 4

The bottom of the bridge is a series of squares that form a rectangle.

1. Glue together four craft sticks to make a square.
2. Glue three more sticks onto the right side of the square to form another square. Repeat. You should have three squares.
3. The bottom is pretty flimsy like this. You can reinforce the structure by adding crossbeams. Add another stick (or more) across each square.

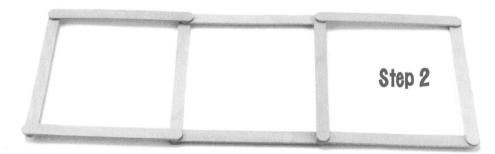

Step 2

continue on next page 11

Let the glue dry on the sides and the bottom of the bridge. After it is dry put the sides and bottom together. You might need someone to hold the bridge while you add the cable ties.

1. Lay the bottom of the bridge on the table.
2. Use zip ties to join the sides to the bottom and each other. The sides should touch at the top like a triangle.

Now you're ready to test your bridge.

1. Place the bridge between the edges of two chairs.
2. Tie rope to the ends of the bridge and let it hang down.
   Tie a small weight to the rope. What happens to the bridge?
3. Keep adding heavier weights. How much can the bridge hold? If the bridge begins to break, how can you change your design? For instance, do you need more crossbeams? More cable ties? Keep testing and evaluating your design.

You don't have to follow this pattern. Try designing your own truss bridge. The key is to use triangles.

EARTHQUAKE-PROOF STRUCTURE

Now that you know a little about making strong structures it's your turn to design your own. Build a tower that can withstand a mini earthquake.

Materials:

- paper and pencil for drawing
- gumdrops
- toothpicks
- table

Steps:

1. Sketch out a structure you think will withstand an earthquake. Try using triangle patterns. You'll test your structure later by shaking the table. Try making the tower at least a foot high.
2. Now start building the **prototype**. Use the gumdrops to hold the toothpicks together to make the building you imagined.
3. Time to test your creation. Shake the table. What happens? Did all or part of the structure fall? How would you make the structure more stable?

4. Redesign and rebuild your building. Give your structure a wider base.
5. Test again! What happened this time? Keep testing and redesigning until you have an earthquake-proof tower. This is what real engineers do!

How it Works:

Larger bases spread out the weight of the building over a larger area. This makes the whole building more stable. Imagine you're standing with your feet together. Someone might easily push you over. But if you stand with your feet apart, you're much harder to push over.

prototype—first trial model of something, made to test and improve the design

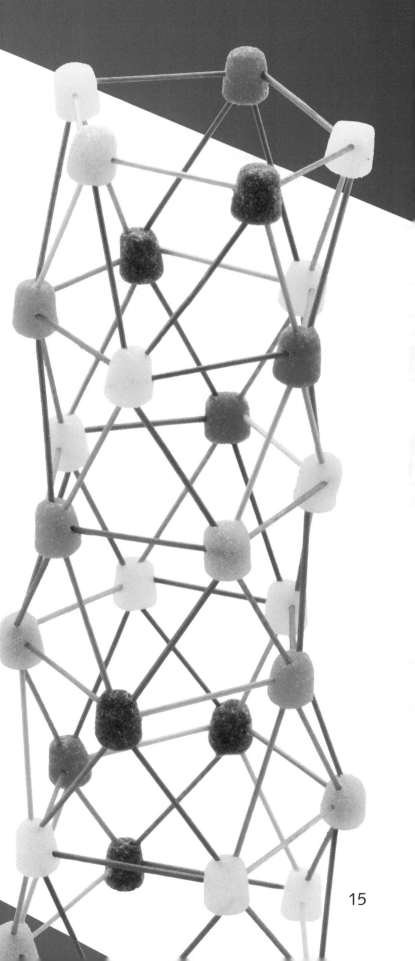

15

WATER FILTER

Many people don't have safe drinking water. **Environmental** engineers try to solve problems like this. They design and build systems to filter out **impurities**. You can design and build a simple filter yourself out of things you probably already have around your house.

Materials:

- potting soil or dirt
- plastic cups
- water
- container (water jug or pitcher)
- plastic water bottle with a cap
- scissors and/or craft knife
- coffee filters
- sand
- gravel
- rocks

Steps:

1. Make some dirty water. Mix about a cup (0.35 grams) of potting soil into a gallon (4.5 liters) of water.
2. Poke a hole in the bottle cap of a plastic water bottle and screw it on the bottle.
3. Ask an adult to help you cut the bottom off of the bottle. Turn the bottle upside down. Rest it in a plastic cup.

Step 3

4. Now let's build the filter out of one or more of these materials: coffee filter, sand, gravel, and/or rocks. Pick one to start with. Pour some into the bottle.

5. Now pour some dirty water into the filter and let it pass through into the plastic cup.

6. What does the water look like? If you used gravel, the water may look gray.

7. Experiment with all of the filter materials. What does the water look like?

8. Try using more than one material, or all of them! Layer one material over another. Put the coarser materials (like rocks or gravel) at the top of the filter.

9. Keep testing and redesigning your filter until you get clear water.

Safety Tip: Don't drink the filtered water. Filtering only removes the dirt and other particles in the water.

How it Works:

Coarse materials, such as gravel and rocks, can stop bigger particles like dirt and twigs from passing through. Finer materials, like sand and the coffee filter, can stop smaller particles.

environmental—relating to the natural world and the impact of human activity on its condition

impurity—something that gets mixed in with another substance

CARDBOARD ARM

A robot arm is a mechanical device that works like a human hand. It can grab and pick up things. Some robot arms look like cranes with a simple claw on the end. Many factories use these to make cars and heavy items. Some robot arms look like a human hand. They use fingers to grasp. This kind of robot arm is trickier to design. Think you can do it? Gather your supplies and get started!

Materials:

- pencil
- cardboard (can be from a box)
- scissors or craft knife
- duct tape

- glue
- plastic straws
- string
- paint/markers (optional)

Step 3

Steps:

1. Draw the outline of a large robot hand and forearm on a piece of cardboard. The hand should be larger than yours, and the forearm should be longer than yours. Tip: You can use just three fingers and a thumb.
2. Cut out the hand and arm with the scissors or craft knife.
3. Unroll a piece of duct tape that is a bit longer that your arm is wide. This is to keep the robot arm on your arm. Fold the tape in half the long way sticky-side to sticky-side. Bend and tape or staple the arm band near the bottom of the robot arm.
4. Bend/crease the fingers and thumbs so that they bend where the knuckles might be. (Tip: look at your own hand. Each finger bends in three places, and the thumb bends in two.) So each finger should have three bendable segments, and the thumb should have two.

5. Cut 16 1-inch-long (2.5 cm) tube pieces out of the straws.

6. Glue a straw tube to the middle of each finger/thumb segment. Also glue a tube on the palm below each finger and thumb.

7. Cut one piece of string for each finger and thumb on your robot. The string should reach from the robot's finger tips to the arm band.

8. Tie a knot in the end of the string and thread it through the straw tubes. Repeat for each finger.

9. Tie a loop in the loose ends of the string for your fingers.

10. Put your arm through the arm band and loop each string over your fingers. You may need to adjust the length of the strings.

11. You should now be able to make the robot fingers move! Test your robot arm. Try moving the fingers and grasping objects. Can you pick up a plastic cup or soda can? If not, what do you need to change in your design? Do you need to shorten the finger strings? Crease the fingers more? Play around with your design until you can pick up an object. You can also decorate your robot arm!

How it Works:

Engineers often study humans or other animals to design robots. This robot hand works a lot like your own. You have a **pulley**-like system inside each finger. The muscle pulls on the **tendon**. The tendon runs through a ring-like band, and makes the finger flex.

pulley—a simple machine made up of a wheel and rope

tendon—a strong, thick cord of tissue that joins a muscle to a bone

PLAY DOUGH CIRCUITS

Electricity can flow through many materials. Most circuits use copper. You experimented with graphite earlier. Now you're going to make electricity flow through play dough! And you get to design your own light-up creation.

Materials:

- play dough
- LED light (5mm)
- 9-volt battery
- battery connector and leads
- modelling clay

Steps:

1. Make two small shapes out of the play dough. Place them close together but don't let them touch.
2. Snap the battery into the battery connector.
3. Stick the positive lead (usually red) into one of the pieces of play dough.
4. Stick the negative lead (usually black) into the other piece.
5. Separate the legs of the LED and stick one into each of the shapes.
6. What happens? The LED should light up. (If it doesn't, flip the LED around.) You have a circuit! You can put other LEDs into this circuit.

Tip: The longer leg of the LED is positive.

7. Now move the two pieces of play dough together. What happens? The LED should go out. This is a short circuit!

8. Separate the shapes again and put a piece of modeling clay between them. What happens now? The light should come back on!

9. Experiment with what you can create. Make a robot with glowing red eyes. Make a car with headlights or a frog with yellow eyes. If your original design doesn't work at first, keep testing and redesigning until it does.

How it Works:

Play dough is a conductor. This means it allows electricity to flow through it. The electricity flows from the battery through the play dough and into the LED. This is a circuit. But electricity likes to take the easiest path. When you push the play dough together, the electricity flows from play dough to play dough. The electricity can't reach the LED. This is called a short circuit. Modeling clay, though, is an **insulator**. When you add it to the circuit, the electricity keeps on moving along the original path.

Tip: You can arrange the play dough circuit in many ways. You can lay your circuits out in lines or circles. Experiment with your circuits and see what you can make.

insulator—a material that keeps electricity inside wires or paths

GLOSSARY

conductor (kuhn-DUHK-tuhr)—a material or object that allows electricity or heat to move through it

dome (DOHM)—a structure shaped like half of a ball

electricity (i-lek-TRI-suh-tee)—flow or stream of charged particles, such as electrons

environmental (in-VY-ruhn-muhnt-uhl)—relating to the natural world and the impact of human activity on its condition

impurity (im-PYOOR-uh-tee)—something that gets mixed in with another substance

insulator (IN-suh-layt-ur)—a material that keeps electricity inside wires or paths

prototype (PROH-tuh-tipe)—first trial model of something, made to test and improve the design

pulley (PUL-ee)—a simple machine made up of a wheel and rope

tendon (TEN-duhn)—a strong, thick cord of tissue that joins a muscle to a bone

truss (TRUHS)—part of a wooden or metal framework, used to support walls, bridges, or a roof

READ MORE

Ardley, Neil. *101 Great Science Experiments.* New York: Dorling Kindersley Limited, Inc., 2014.

Dahl, Oyvind. *Electronics for Kids.* San Francisco: No Starch Press, 2016.

Latham, Donna. *Bridges and Tunnels.* Build It Yourself. White River Junction, Ver.: Nomad Press, 2012.

INTERNET SITES

Use FactHound to find Internet sites related to this book.

Visit *www.facthound.com*

Just type in 9781515768845 and go.

Check out projects, games and lots more at
www.capstonekids.com

INDEX